15 Minute Principle

"If you do what you've always done, you'll get what you've always gotten."

–Tony Robbins

15 Minute Principle

**Taking You From Where You Are to Where
You Want to Be in Just 15 Minutes**

Michael Brue

Florida

15 Minute Principle

Copyright © 2018 Michael Brue

All rights reserved.

Tiger Storm Press

1391 NW St Lucie West Blvd, Suite 247

Port St Lucie, FL 34986

TigerStormPress.com

ISBN-10: 0692132600
ISBN-13: 978-0692132609

Published in the United States of America

Dedication

I would like to dedicate this book to CrossFit Jupiter, which was the birthplace of my 15 Minute Principle. My greatest metaphysical growth came from my greatest physical self. My son Jules Matthew Brue was later one of the first test studies for my 15 Minute Principle. A special acknowledgement to CrossFit Jupiter as a catalyst and a strong shout out to my son Jules for teaching me things that Life itself could not. My wife Angelique Brue later decided to buy CrossFit Jupiter after herself becoming dedicated to CrossFit, she was so committed to working out, she was still doing CrossFit at 7 months pregnant with our 3rd child. She went back as soon as the doctor cleared her after the birth.

"Dream big and dare to fail."

–Norman Vaughan

What Others Say About Working With Michael

"I have been a fan since you hired me back in 2006. Your energy and fighting inspiration have made me the Realtor© I am today. I remember our meetings where you gave me the "you can do it" talks, and still think of them today. You were young and new to KW but with an old and knowledgeable big spirit. You're the best Mike."

AnnMarie Minervini

"There's no doubt that you've had the most positive impact on my life. When I walked into your office over five years ago, I was filled with fear that I would not be able to start a new career in my 40s. I shared with you a little bit about my past accomplishments and my tenacity to succeed and it instantly struck a chord with you. You spent the next 30 minutes getting to know me and seeing my unlimited potential. You didn't just fill my head with clichés about success. You personalized a plan encouraged me to follow the steps to attain my goals.

Within a short time, I closed my first few deals and began teaching classes at Keller Williams. You made me feel part of the family at a time of transition where I could've felt lost. Over the years, you've encouraged me through the crisis, motivated me to persevere and now I'm happy to say that I am thriving in a career that I've grown to love. I never imagined that in my late 40s I would've found my true career path and a dear friend who shares many of the same philosophies and passion for life. I will forever be grateful for Your ability to always see the best in me and quite actually, the best in everyone. I truly consider you a blessing in my life. You are one of a kind, Michael!"

Michelle Burke

"My personal experience with Michael Brue has been one of a kind and generous person focused on promoting the success and well-being of all. An incredibly energetic professional always thinking outside the box to provide his agents great ideas. Most of all, I think he may be the most loving, sensitive father I have ever known. Grateful to be a dad and proud so show it."

Marguerite B. Krute

"Great men and women inspire those around them to live out their greatness. Michael Brue has a power that few possess, an inner confidence that is intentionally focused on seeing others succeed. Michael is never too busy for a call or text and provides value wherever he goes. Always looking for the Win/Win solution, he has guided me through some challenging situations. He balances family life and work life tremendously. His walk matches his talk, with a high value on Integrity. Thank you for inspiring me!"

Tammy Werthem

"My first meeting with Michael Brue...

It was the summer of 2004 and I remember it like it was yesterday. My mother and I were a very successful team at Coldwell Banker and we were content. It was my mother's 32nd year as a Realtor© and it was my 16th year. My dad had recently retired, and my mom was close to retiring too. We were referred the best-selling author, pastor and motivational speaker, Dr. John Maxwell as a buyer. We were both very excited to meet him and help him with the perfect home in the Palm

Beaches. At the same time, several agents in our office switched to the new broker in town, Keller Williams. I didn't know much about them, but I was convinced to meet with Mike the team leader. I was led to Mike's office with expectations of just another broker that wanted more agents. I quickly realized that Mike is like no one else I've ever met. He was surprisingly passionate about life and Keller Williams. The more he told me, the more skeptical I became. I didn't see how any company could fulfill such promises and expectations. I remember thinking that if just one of Mike's many claims were true, I would have to join KW. I joined and then broke the news to my mother/business partner. She was devastated and didn't know how I could do this to her. Later that day she was showing the property to Dr. Maxwell and she told him what happened. He asked what company I went to. When she said Keller Williams, he very enthusiastically replied "touchdown" with raised arms in the shape of goal posts. He said he knew Gary Keller personally and was the key note speaker at one of the family reunions. He confidently told my mother to join me at KW right away. Fourteen years later, I realize that every claim Mike made at the first meeting was absolutely accurate and some were understated, and my mother is still working with me! Thank you, Mike, for meeting me and improving my life and career!"

Scott D. Smith, PA

Keller Williams Realty Palm Beaches

"Michael, the true you is not the hard exterior you choose for the world to see. It is not truly the pit bull bully dog. The true you is a passionate caring individual whose passion is sometimes mistaken for arrogance because those people don't possess that type of inner fire cannot see past their own jealousies. The true you has very few in your inner circle and some that believe they are however there are only there for a special purpose or short period of time. The true you loves deeply your family and your faith. The true you doesn't show fear because you analyze it and then conquer it. "

I appreciate the true you because strong people are people to learn from and cherish as a leader."

Cristi Hernandez

"Michael Brue impacted my life before we ever had the chance to speak one on one. I had always considered myself to be a strong leader, but at the time was struggling due to the loss of multiple close family members. Michael came to speak to our office one day and that is when I saw a Leader of Leaders, a man respected and looked up to by everyone in the room. It wasn't what he said that day, but his presence, a motivating and inspirational force that hit me at my core. It was then that I knew, that I did not just want to be an agent, but part of his leadership team, I finally found the Leader, I had been searching for, for years. Since that day Michael has continued to be that Leader and my own leadership abilities have grown exponentially through his guidance. Thank you, Michael."

Steve Banasiak

"Michael, I will be forever grateful for you believing in me! If it were not for you, I would not be where I am in my career in Real Estate today. You take the time to really listen and your advice has always guided me in the right direction. You are not only my Mentor, I consider you to be a valued friend and I am happy to have you in my life! Inspiring and Leading others in a positive direction is a special trait that you have mastered, and I speak for a multitude of people whose lives you have touched. Keep on being you, you are one of a kind!

This was harder than I thought. I kept running on and on this is the version that sums it all up! Thank you for being you!"

Dawn Mansur, PA

"I know Michael Brue as my broker, my mentor, a true involved leader, a coach, a person who inspires everyone he knows, and a person who has my total respect and admiration. I must admit I love Facebook for many reasons, but when I see a post from Michael, I read it. No, not just look at it, but read it and interpret it for my benefit. I know that each and every word is there to encourage and build better, happier, more effective lives. But by far the most important thing I have learned about Michael is he is a real person. A husband, a proud father and a good son and family person. And for me, he is a friend. He tries to help and encourage and his follow through is right on target. He makes everyone feel important. It is with gratitude and appreciation that I take this time to express these thoughts."

Betty Welch

"*The General* AKA Michael Brue! Truly the most influential person I have ever met! I met him at a very low part of my life. He quickly became my friend and mentor. He believed in me, encouraged me, motivated me when I didn't have the strength or energy to drive forward. One of my favorite quotes from him, "Give me the 30 second version". He is full of Passion, Drive, and most important Integrity. I am forever grateful to have this extraordinary man in my life!

Thank you for continuing to guide me to Break thru the next level."

Kellie Linder

Table of Contents

Introduction

"Whatever the mind of man can conceive and believe, it can achieve." – Napoleon Hill

Welcome to the **15 Minute Principle**.

In order for me to share with you properly how my 15 Minute Principle changed my life and undoubtedly it can also change yours. I must first take you back to my real estate career as it began as a broker of record and leader of a little company known as KW Palm Beaches. I started my career as a Realtor© in the year 2000. I had just turned 25 and what I realized pretty quick, as a small-town kid who grew up pretty poor in Syracuse, NY, was that if I was going to make it big in this lifetime then it would be up to me to figure it out. I knew I had better do that quickly, especially in a strictly commission-based line of work as it would determine if I would eat or not that week. If we fast forward through the struggles of the first years in general real estate to my last full year in real estate sales I was on track to close about $200,000 in GCI (Gross Commission Income).

And as the year was quickly coming to an end I was having the time of my life. Notwithstanding the fact that I mentally quit about seven times in my first two years. I thought to myself, not bad for a kid from a broken home who had to grow up fast from the school of hard knocks to living in paradise. I mean come on 3 years later in 2003, I was making good money living in South Florida at 28 years old, and my life was pretty much a party all the time.

Something else very big happened that year, my son was born in December 2003. Well, that certainly changed the game. Although I wasn't looking for change, in late 2003 I was recruited to Keller Williams Realty of the Palm Beaches by a guy named Charles Posess. He wanted me to become their Broker/ Team

Leader of that office. At the time, I respectfully said no thanks a handful of times, but he was relentless, and something happened in that last meeting. Here's a note on our story that may perfectly portray our new business relationship at that time. One of the first things we did together was attend a regional leadership meeting.

One of the things that happened at the leadership meeting is they went over the stats of all the market centers (Real Estate Offices) that were in the South Florida Region for Keller Williams. We were dead last in every category. At that moment I leaned over to him and said: "I don't like being last, we won't be here for long." He simply smiled and nodded. Now the truth about this recruiting strategy was not all palm trees and sunsets. I make a lot of movie references, so if you don't particularly watch movies, you're probably not going to get all of me. If you do, you'll love this.

Do you remember the movie "The Karate Kid" with Ralph Macchio? There was a really cool part of that movie, where Daniel (Ralph Macchio) moved with his mom to Reseda, CA. The picture that he was painted from his mom and the brochure was of beautiful ice blue pools, palm trees blowing, and gorgeous people at the beaches in bikinis. When he finally arrives there, the pool is green, it's got about a foot of brown water in the pool, and I think there were frogs jumping. They go to open the curtains for the window in the kitchen and there's no view of the ocean. It's actually a brick wall. That's how I felt when I came to Keller Williams back in late 2003. When I got there, I was painted this grandeur picture from Charles Posses. He was laying it down pretty thick, and he was recruiting me to come join him. I think he even said back then "We're going to dominate the real estate market together."

Then I get there I immediately want to look at the stats. We found out we were number 22 out of 22. Dead last in every single category. That means we sold the least number of units, we sold the least amount of volume, and we were the smallest office in size. I thought it would be best to start you with our story because it's relevant to what I'm going to be sharing with you in this book. I realized that this story, this process is the gift that people ask me for all the time. I am always asked:

"How did you guys do this?" Here is the short version of how we made the magic happen.

I was 28 and arguably some would have even said I was absolutely nuts. I was pretty much out of my mind and I was determined never to really grow up. In late 2003 I agreed to meet Charles. Something interesting about Charles is that he is a real estate attorney. I didn't think I'd like him at all going into this first meeting where he was asking me if I would like to become the Broker/ Team Leader of KW Palm Beaches. Now he may read this book one day, so I should probably quickly divert to, he won me over and he was actually a pretty cool guy, and he was the real deal. Worth big money, but so down to earth, an actual self-made man.

I did go into that last meeting with him reluctantly, because I said to myself: "There's no way that this guy and I are ever going to come to terms on anything, let alone see eye to eye, how could we possibly even like each other." I literally went into that meeting with a notepad and a script that I practiced telling him, "Thank you so much for the opportunity, but no thank you."

Obviously, that script didn't work. I never even got to pull that note card out and give that speech, because something weird happened in the middle of our last meeting and we just kind of connected. We are the absolute odd couple. If there were a real-life Felix and Oscar, we would fit the bill. No one could believe that we were going to be successful and make it together a year let alone over a decade.

Thinking back, there might have been bets on who was going to kill each other first that year. I can't tell you exactly what it was, but I think I learned what it was later. It wasn't something that I could pick up that day. I went in to give him the whole speech of saying, listen, I'm at Re/Max, and I'm making a couple hundred thousand dollars a year. Life is good. My wife is pregnant, she was carrying my first child and it was going to be a boy. You can imagine how high on life I was. I was walking around like I was six foot six, 280 pounds of ripped muscle like I could walk through walls on a daily basis.

I said yes, and the rest was history. When we got started we had about twenty-five real estate agents in total.

Of the twenty-five, only five of them had sold real estate. A far cry from today where most of my agents are celebrating their best months ever. When I ask a classroom today to tell me what is happening with their deals, I almost always get agents telling me that they listed a couple of homes in the first few months or they have sales coming in from helping buyers find homes. Most of the time we have more real estate going on in the room in two minutes than my whole crew had put on the board in the eight months they were open prior to our joining forces in the Palm Beaches. Just so we are on the same page as to what I was facing with this uphill climb. We literally had 25 real estate agents and 20 of them had never listed or sold a home before.

Now let me fast forward through a lot of pain, pleasure, and passion that we don't have time to get into and all the crazy stuff that had to happen back then. That's going to be in the next book that's the real, raw, authentic truth, so you will have to buy that book once its published to hear those stories. We just commonly called all that growth.

Through the pain we ended up growing from 25 agents in 2003 to in 2018 we have more than 1,100 plus agents. We have grown from one office, one market center, one company, to now we have five market centers, two business centers with seven total locations. Our last location that opened is on the beach in Vero Beach, Florida. Our footprint now includes KW Palm Beaches, KW Jupiter, KW Treasure Coast, KW Palm City, KW Port St Lucie, KW Vero Beach and KW Vero Luxury Beachside.

We are often asked, how did you guys do it? How did you climb in agent count, volume sold, and units sold for over a decade straight and marched right through a downturn in the market? Something powerful happens when you put your focus on something that you really want. Not only did we become the largest group of offices in size on the eastern seaboard for Keller Williams, but we also become the largest in size of singly owned offices by one individual or one group of people on the eastern seaboard of Florida. We're not just the largest, we have sold and closed over $1.5 billion in sales over the last 12 trailing months from April 2018. This puts us in the number one pole position for units by far more than that of our closest competitor from Palm Beach to Vero Beach!

If you try to chart our growth in each category you will find lines that go up for as far back as you can track. There's a huge gap for sure between where we are today and where our competitors from yesteryear went. I believe the real estate landscape has been totally changed. I don't believe we are without competitors, I just strongly believe my new competitors are just not here yet.

In the rest of this book I'm going to share with you the absolute thing that I think changed our whole business trajectory. I have a couple cool ways to break it down for you. Let's get started.

Lead Generation

What is the number one thing that a real estate agent must do to get into this business and start making money?

If you said lead creation / generation, then you are correct.

I want to break lead creation / generation down for you in 30 seconds. You ready? Whether you are brand new, you've been around for five or six years and you're still trying to figure it out, or whether you've been around for 10 years and you're a ninja and you could disappear so that people can't even see you anymore, then this is for you. We must as agents make contact with the outside world in a very systematic, a very specific way so that it leads to appointments with people. This is how I break it down in a very simplistic manner. I start out with three boxes. The first one is for contacts, the second one is for appointments, and the third one is for signed contracts.

Lead generation to me is fundamentally boiled down to these three things. Are you ready?

1. You must make contact with a certain number of people every day you are in business.

2. Those contacts will lead to a certain number of appointments for buyers, sellers, renters or investors.

3. Then based on your presentation skillset, your interaction of relationship building and your

ability to get people to say YES, you will ultimately get a certain number of contracts signed. It could be for a listing agreement or a buyer making an offer on a house.

We want to get sellers, buyers, and renters to say yes. With the ultimate goal that we want is that those listings, leases and buyer contracts move forward down through the steps of actual closings because that's how you make money in real estate. Side note fact, this is universal for all sales, real estate, mortgage, insurance etc.

When I coach somebody, the first thing I ask them is:

How many contacts are you making with the outside world that are potentially people that you could turn into contracts?

You can do this with me right now, take out a piece of paper and a pen and draw these three boxes on it. I'll wait, go ahead and grab your paper and pen.

The first box is how many contacts are you making on a daily basis. These are with people who want to potentially do one of the following four things when it comes to real estate:

- Buy
- Sell
- Lease
- Invest

And on the investment one, because if you're stumped and you're not sure what to talk about or what to say, or maybe who your audience is, almost everybody in your sphere of influence is or could be an investor. Your parents are investors, your siblings are investors. Your neighbors could be investors. Anyone and everyone you touch and see every day could potentially invest in real estate. Is real estate a good investment, yes or no?

Oh yeah! I happen to find it to be a really good investment.

Now we know that you must make a certain number of contacts. If I make zero contacts and I tell absolutely no one that I'm in real estate, if I don't talk to anybody the whole entire week, what is the probability that I'm going to have appointments with people? You got it right, Zero!

Let's flip that. Let's say that I make 50 contacts and I'm not really that good yet. Let's say that I've got to get better. And by the way, when I first came into this, I came into this on the sales side of the business, I sounded like one of the (Jerky Boys). I don't know if you ever heard of them or remember who that was you can Google it for a good laugh. To put it simply, I was real rough around the edges. Which means not everybody liked me when I would talk to them on the phone. I think I had one guy say to me you should probably never make phone calls.

Let's get back to our example. If I need 50 and I'm not that good and I'm a little rough around the edges or I'm just getting started and I finally get to the point where I make 50 contacts, what is my probability of making appointments? Certainly, better than the zero we had before, right. For the sake of this example and from what I have seen from new agents who are just getting started, having a 10% conversion is ok. That would mean out of the 50 contacts, I would get 5 appointments.

Now, what happens after I get 5 appointments with people who are buyers, sellers, investors or renters? Even if we are new and we are rough around the edges, we go on those 5 appointments. What could potentially happen if I had at least 5 appointments with real people who want to go out and look at properties? They could be looking to rent, to buy, to sell their own home, maybe a FSBO (For Sale By Owner), or even an investor looking to purchase more properties for their portfolio. Let me ask you this, do you live in a house, townhome or condo? We pretty much all do unless you live on a boat or something cool like that.

For the most part, everybody is either a buyer or a seller, investor or renter at some point. And it's kind of neat but we all have a sphere of influence, which is our people, our system, and our personal network. And those people who are connected to us could be right now having discussions about buying a new home or buying a bigger home. Maybe actually buying less of a home. Maybe they're getting divorced. Maybe they're having a baby. Maybe they're having two babies. They just found out, man we've got twins. Bam, now we need two more bedrooms right. Or maybe it's not so pretty and nice and sometimes no baby. They're downsizing because of a loss.

The point is all these conversations are happening right now, I promise you. Each one of you has people who have a network and a system out there that these discussions are happening and if you're not in the game, you're not one of the people that are lined up that could be in position for those opportunities to help your people and you won't get those contracts. What I really want to do today is just move you into making it possible for you to have an opportunity that could be sitting right in front of you.

If I had a certain number of appointments lined up, like we said, if we had 5 and maybe I'm new, so I'm not that good yet, how many contracts can I possibly get? What's the lowest probable ratio here? I could get zero, but let's say that I can even get one. Most people are going to be able to close 1 out of 5 deals. For you seasoned ninjas, you should be in the range of 8 out of 10 because most of your business is personal referrals, so if you are following along, up your percentages. For this diagram let's just keep it real realistic.

CONTACTS		APPOINTMENTS		CONTRACTS
50	-	5	-	1

You can do this, you're amazing. I believe in you, out of your 50 contacts, you made 5 appointments for the week and you get 1 signed contract. If you can repeat this for 50 weeks a year that's 50 contracts a year. Of course, assuming everyone wants to take two weeks of vacation a year. Now there is something really cool about appointments. Appointments can give residual ones. Let me explain this a little further for you. This week you had 5 appointments. One of those guys and gals are going to say yes, even if you are not that good just because you are trying. Some people may even give you an "I feel bad for you", like a sympathy appointment. The point is taking the action to put you in the game.

But what could happen in week two is you can get another appointment from the previous week's activity. It's called residual. Maybe you talked to a for sale by owner, they weren't really ready then. You talked to them, you actually follow up and you call them more than once. In two weeks from now, you catch them when they say "Man, I've really got to sell this property. Before I didn't really want to sell the home, I wasn't sure I wanted to sell it but now she's driving me crazy. We need to sell the home." Then they say the magic music to my ears question. "When can you come to our home?"

Can you see how the no from the initial contact can lead to a residual appointment? It's called follow through. When you put the energy into a contact you should continue working with that contact until one of three things happen.

1. You list the home

2. They sell the home

3. They list with someone else

If number 3 happens, then you immediately say, "You have made a great decision, I wish you all the best, I'm sure you chose a fantastic agent if whatever reason that does not work out feel free to save my number." Always take the high road and follow supreme ethics, it will pay dividends you can't see into the future.

Let's kick things up a notch here and look at what happens if I make 100 calls and contacts. I get in touch with 100 contacts of people who want to buy, sell, lease and invest.

If I continue doing what I did on the first 50, what would my numbers look like now? Out of the 100 contacts, I might set 10 appointments now. If I set 10 maybe instead of getting one plus a residual one I could get two plus maybe a residual two. You can play with the numbers and we can look at that all day and you get it. It just makes sense. Business begins when you start taking action and can only multiply from there.

This is a system that can be used by people who do any kind of sales whatsoever. How many contacts do you make on a weekly basis?

When I'm coaching an agent and I ask, "So let's start with you telling me how many contacts do you make daily?" If they answer "ah, zero, I don't really make contacts." I'm not sure I'm going to be able to help them until I get them to make contacts. The first step is making contacts, so people know you exist. If you are hiding you can't close deals and get paid.

Now if you implement this and you are having trouble with making 50 contacts and getting 5 appointments, then we need to look deeper at what is going on. What we would look at next would be not necessarily what they are saying, but it could be in how they are saying it. It might just be an adjustment. Have you ever had a conversation with somebody that it wasn't what they said, it was how they said it? It could be the tonality of it and when they said it, you were like, really. It automatically put you on the defense and you couldn't have a good conversation from there because you just didn't like the way it was laid out. It wasn't what they said, it was how they said it. Be conscious of this.

Here is a great technique that I use with my students that you can use to help you get more appointments and increase your conversion rate. Sometimes internally we think we are doing and saying the right thing, but sometimes on the outside, it is not perceived that way. I will sit with my students and just listen to their calls. Not so much what they are saying, but more the tone of the call. What you can do is ask one of your office partners or someone in the office who you trust their opinion to sit in on some of your calls. Just ask for honest feedback on how you deliver your message and then make any changes that could help you improve. We can all get better at everything and having constructive criticism is a great way to improve quickly. Be open to this, it's called growth.

Now I have broken down a simple formula that you can use to start lead generating today, but I know that some people will still not take action and I know why. I am going to give you the excuse you can use right now. You ready? Here it is.

The greatest excuse why most people legitimately can't lead generate today is because you don't know who you're contacting. You don't know who to call. You don't know who you should actually be communicating with.

That's legit. Let's remove this excuse so you can no longer use it. Because I just gave you the excuse. Now we're going to remove the excuse. So after today, you can't use this excuse. You must think of a better one. But here's the excuse I want to get away from. I don't know who to call. I'm not sure who to communicate with. I'm not going to make contacts today because I just don't know who to contact. In the next chapter, I am going to break it down for you so that we can remove this excuse from your vocabulary for good. Essentially the best way is to make a list the night before and block the time to get through that list.

Time Blocking

The first thing I need you to do is decide what time of day you should make outbound contacts. What would be the best time? Now, I don't necessarily want to know when you're in prime time. Some of you are at prime time at midnight. I get that, sometimes at night, I'm on fire too. If you feel that you are best in off hours just keep in mind what would be the best time to reach people about business.

When you're on is not necessarily the best time to do the whole block of time. It is when you know that you have to get it done so that you can't evade it and you can't not do it. Because here's how it works for me. If I personally don't set this up at the onset of my business day and the first thing that I'm going to do, then I probably won't do it that day. And here's why I won't do it. Because I'll roll in about 8:00ish and get my coffee. Coffee and I, we've got a thing. Then I have to be somewhat social. Are you social? Sometimes too social, kind of like a social butterfly. You know, you move around wanting to find out what's going on. Who did what fun last night, etc. So, I always consciously look to put being social after lead generation. It can be a reward for some of us.

Here's what happens most days if you don't make lead generation first. The distraction and excuses take on a role of the first position. It starts with you saying to yourself, even though I need to start my lead generation now, I'll start it in a little bit from now. I'm going to do it in a half an hour from now. And you'll sit down in a half an hour and then you'll think, oh, this is kind of right before lunch now.

So, then you think, I'll go to lunch now too since everyone else is at lunch they don't want to be bothered before eating either. Now I'm going to wait to do my lead generation until right after lunch. I need to eat too, right. You see this just leads to more excuses. I'm going to have a full belly when I come back, and I'll think again, oh, I don't want to make calls right now because I feel full. If I feel full, everyone I could call is probably feeling full too. I'll just do it in a little bit.

Ok in a little bit, right before everybody goes home, that's a great time. I'm going to call then. And then that time would roll around and I'll check some emails and do some Facebook and text with some friends and send some emojis. Then that time will come, and I'll think, you know, people are getting ready to go home. I don't really want to bother them right now because I don't want to be bothered right now and yeah, that's probably not a good time. So then you know what I'll just do, I'll just do it in a little while. Let them get home, get relaxed and then I'll call.

Then that time will come and at that time I'm think once again, I don't really feel like making calls. I don't want to be called. If I don't want to take calls at this hour, who's going to want to get a call from me.

And this will continue into the next day. Then it will just keep going. I don't know if you're anything like me, whether you are a lot or little then this might apply to you too. I must just do it at the beginning of the day. Just do it first and get it done!

Time blocking is a part of the plan. I would take my calendar and plan for the entire year.

> **TIP:** I would start time blocking days off and vacation time, because who doesn't like taking time off. Once you're in a rhythm with blocking time switch to lead creation / generating time.

I would put in there my lead generation time block first thing at the onset of every business day. Block time for initial contact, for following up, for actual setting appointments, for working on the business. I also color coded my appointments in my calendar. Orange, by the way, was recurring appointments. Then of course green would be time for actual new appointments for new/follow up. Do what's best for your personal schedule, but I personally always had two morning appointment times and then I always had three in the afternoon. I had five in the day. So, if there are five days in a week and there are five possible appointments for a day, I would have 25 possibilities of opportunity each and every week.

Oh, and by the way, 12:00 was always yellow. That is lunch. I had to schedule lunch because often, I'll forget to eat because I would get caught up being social or busy helping people, so, I would just forget to eat. Here's what happened when I had my calendar in front of me. It would help keep me purposeful making outbound contact for those appointments, always looking to fill the vacant appointment spots. Do you see the psychology in this? Through the discipline of maintaining this routine and already having the calendar coded helped me stay focused on simply filling in times with actual named appointments.

When I would talk to somebody I'd say "I'd love to meet you tomorrow. I have two openings. I can meet at 11:00 or 1:00. What's better for you?" What was my main focus? Yes! I was trying to fill my days, weeks and month with appointments. In the beginning, this is like a workout routine, it starts with making the commitment to the time, showing up, dress the part and making it through the workout. You get results after the routine becomes a habit. It becomes something you do constantly without thinking of excuses anymore.

When I am coaching people at first, I'm not looking for results I am simply looking for the action taken. I don't really care about anything else except for booking appointments. I have even said I need you to take action, I just want you to focus on setting the appointments. I need you to go screw up a little bit today. Some of you are way too perfect. I need you to go figure out how to just book a couple of appointments. Sometimes the best thing you can do to learn is to mess up a few attempts at setting appts with buyers and some sellers.

> **"The fastest way to learn is to take the action."**
> BRUE

The fastest way to learn is to take the action that gets you to a place to self-discover what you did wrong, so you can now figure out what can you say to make it go right. I want you to go on a lot of appointments because it is through the many attempts that you will begin to get better. I want you to start today and commit to a number of appointments that you can mentally agree you could go on in a week.

Now what happens if somebody says I can't meet you at 11:00 or 1:00 at all, neither of those work, what do you say? You can say, "Well, actually I'm glad you brought that up because those earlier times were ideal for me so that's why I was suggesting those, but I also have an opening at 3:00 and another at 5:00. Do either one of those work for you?" Because remember, I'm looking at my calendar, I'm trying to fill up all the appointment spots because I know that if I can get 20 to 25 appointments booked for the week things are going to be amazing. It's important to me to be in the top 1% of whatever it is that I am committed to doing.

Think about your number and what's realistic for you, 5-10-15 appointments a week. If you hit your goal number of appointments a week of people who want to buy, sell, lease or invest, you will be on track to hit your goals. I'm going to tell you right now, I don't even care if English isn't your first language. You're going to be in my top 1% if you can book 20 to 25 appointments a week with prospects.

It doesn't matter where you are at with your appointment number goal, just start today and start with creating the map by time blocking your calendar for the entire year with pre-set appointment times.

> ## "Don't just try, do!"
>
> **BRUE**

Don't just try, do! You will naturally get better because you're actually running around with people, you're talking to people, you're chatting with people and you're building relationships. You're finding out what they say, what makes sense, who needs what and how can you help them. Maybe you will even learn what you shouldn't say anymore. Oh, I think I might have offended that guy or I think I was a little too harsh, Maybe I was too opinionated. Perhaps you were moving a little too quick rushing through the call. You probably call it other things, but I call it, oh I was moving a little too quickly. I noticed I could slow it down a little bit and probably benefit from doing so. This is called, getting better.

Over time you're going to get better. I don't care how many appointments you go on. The goal is always to block your time, make sure that lead generation is the first thing on your calendar. The first thing when you're going to step into your day, just so you don't create excuses around it. If you stand on it, you say this is what I'm going to do, this is how I'm going to do it, this is it and you block out everything else. Listen I have friends that I love too. Real friends know to respect your building time, they will be there after you are done. You know those friends you would take a bullet for, you know real friends the ones you can have drinks with, you can cuss with, we can simply call them real friends. I'm not talking about social media friends. I am talking about friends that love you and would take a bullet for you. But they know don't contact me during my lead generation time. That's protected lead creation/ business building time. You need to keep respect on this time and share when that time is with everyone because that's how you bring everyone around you into helping with your business goals.

Now, right after that protected time is done, you can reward yourself with being as social as you want to be. Go ahead and hear about everything that is going on. Fill your social bucket. Jump back on social media!

> ## "Starve your distractions and feed your focus."
>
> **BRUE**

Starve your distractions and feed your focus. All the things that divert your focus are taking your energy. Remain laser focused on getting those appointments. You can even warm up with an affirmation. "Every time I make calls, I set appointments." You see how this natural focus takes care of itself? So now I want to take the next step. Without further ado, here is my 15 Minute Principle.

15 Minute Principle

My 15 Minute Principle didn't come to me through business. This is a little bit of a disclosure, perhaps a bit of a disclaimer. I am sure you have heard of a gym or maybe even you are a member of one now. You might be paying 12-month membership fees right now and have not gone but a couple of times this past year. Trust me, I'm guilty of the same. I had a fight with LA Fitness about 10 years ago. I paid them $750 for three years all at once and then I didn't go. Then I went in, and I asked for some of my $750 back. They said, no that's gone. It didn't go in my favor. But anyway, I'm

going to tell you, I've been in and out of the gym my whole life trying this or that physical goal.

Here's the reality about the gym. I don't know what your situation is, I know everybody's a little different. And by the way, I don't care if you ever go to a gym. I'll love you the way you are, and I think you're absolutely perfect so please don't change, unless you want to for you. But, if you do want to change something, usually it's a physical something, you need to do some level of exercise.

It could be as simple as walking on the beach. I think they've scientifically proven, doctors have said it, that a body in motion stays in motion. So, you've got to be doing something so that you stay young and healthy for as long as possible. If there's somebody in your life that you need to take care of, you've got to make sure that you take care of yourself first. Just like on a plane, they say to put the oxygen mask on yourself first, so you can put it on the children and other people.

I decided that the way I would stay in motion was to start CrossFit. CrossFit is one of the new craze in workouts today. It is like military style boot camp with multiple exercises that combine body weight and free weights with gymnastics. It mainly consists of varied functional movements performed at high intensity. This isn't a pitch for CrossFit. You don't need to do CrossFit to get this message, but for me, this is where I found my 15 Minute Principle.

On the very first day I went to CrossFit I quit the very first day. I said to myself: "There is no way." I thought I was in pretty good shape. I had been training my whole life in some way or form. I went the first day and after they blew the whistle I literally thought I was having a heart attack. I haven't felt like that since the high school gym locker room where they make you do way too much weight and I felt like I was going to throw up. I literally was fighting it back the whole way down the road as I drove away. I just couldn't let them see me get sick.

It was just a new experience I kept telling myself, so I did go back the next day. I think I went back because I was stubborn. I'm going back to CrossFit because there was no way that I would let them see me quit. Yep, I ended up quitting every day. Swear to God, every single day for the first 30 days. I kept saying to myself: "This is not for me, this is for other people. This is crazy. I'm not doing this!" But I got through my first 30 days and something happened. I said to myself: "You know what, I can do this, and I didn't die today!" That has been my mantra ever since. I didn't tell anybody that, but privately when I was driving home in my car I'd say out loud I didn't die. Yes. I'm still alive. We're still moving forward. I started to see the gifts of the results.

This is where I got this gift. This is where it came to me chemically seeped through my physical self. I didn't get this piece through my metaphysical self. I got this through my physical self. Two years later, at the time I was in the best shape of my life. When I first started CrossFit I could not do one pullup without a band. I should probably never tell you that. Maybe I just lost my cool card, but that's the truth, I could not pull my body weight up without using a band. That was really hard for me. I went home, and I would say to myself: "I need a lot of work. I need this for me."

I want to tell you today, I probably could go outside, and do about 30 pull ups military strict style in a row before I fall down. So, about two years later I get in the absolute best shape of my life. I was turning 40. I am pretty darn certain that my 40-year-old self could knock my 20-year-old self out if he shows up knocking on this door. Just in case that ever happens, that's important. Something happened through this change. I never worked out more than 15 minutes a day for those two years. It literally took me longer to drive to the gym than it did to actually do the workout completely.

"You can do ANYTHING
for 15 minutes"

BRUE

From all of this, I got the 15 Minute Principle. I said you can do anything for 15 minutes. You can probably be tortured for 15 minutes. I know, because I was tortured every day by these CrossFit coaches. That's what it felt like for the first 30 days anyway. I tell you this, not so you run out and grab a CrossFit membership, but to inspire you to realize that you can commit to anything for 15 minutes and see it through. Anything!

One day I said to myself, wait a minute. 15 minutes. This changed my whole physical self. It changed my whole life. And people are always now complimenting me on this or that along with everything else. It was really weird the first year I was in CrossFit. Some days I would come around the corner and I might see Roger and he'd say, "Wow Brue, you look swole. You look big. You look thick. You look good!" And I would say, "Yeah. It's awesome, right?" Then I walked around the other corner and Jake would too say, "Wow, what's up man, you look thin today. You look really skinny. Are you losing a lot of weight?" And I would reply, "Man, same day, same outfit, two different people!" What's going on?

I think what it was is that your body is moving everything around as you are making changes. Because here's something cool. Two years later I weigh the exact same weight that I did when I started. It's just all in different places and moved all around. Starting with 15 minutes a day can and will change your life.

Now that I had the 15 Minute Principle, I had another challenge happen. My challenge is I have a 14-year-old son and his name is Jules. He's beautiful, he's really tall, he's handsome, he is built like a little muscle machine. But he wasn't always this tall. He's 14 now at the time of this book being published. I remember when he was only half this size and he was developing along the way.

Let me take you back to when he was seven years old and he was in baseball. He was having the time of his life, but, he could not hit the ball to save his life. This was probably the most painful season of my life. You have to understand this. I am super competitive, and yes, I am that dad. The problem was that my son could not hit the ball. I tried everything. We tried private lessons. We had batting coaches. We took him to the in-line batting cages that were inside. I had a coach coming to the field to work with him the day or evening of the game. Nothing worked, he just couldn't hit the ball.

It wasn't something physical, it was psychological. I actually had one coach come to the game one night. I asked when Jules goes up to bat just go get in his head. And every time he'd get up to bat, he'd get up there and he'd do his thing. He looked great. He looked so cool in his uniform, but no matter what, every single time he would strike out. Then there was me cheering from the stands "Come on Jules, you just got to see the ball, just put your eyes on this ball." I was literally going crazy here guys. It wasn't one game. It was a whole season.

I remember at one game I was with my Mom, Deborah Claflin, she's no longer with us anymore, so this was a special moment that I had with her. She's sitting there on the bench with me and I put my arm around her and I asked "Ma, did I ever strike out when I was little?" As she leaned into me, she looked right in my face and said "this is going to hurt, but no, never Michael. You could bat left handed and right handed at 5 years old, your father worked with you every day since you could even hold a bat." I said okay Mom. So, I'm thinking paternity test, just kidding! I just couldn't understand what's going on. Here is what I did. I tried everything. I threw money at lessons and I threw coaches at him left and right, I did everything that any great, competitive, crazy father would do. None of it worked. What did I do? I said I'm going to try using the 15 Minute Principle thing on him and see what happens.

I called my boss Charles Posess and said look, I'm leaving work every day at 5:00 because I'm going to go home, I'm going to spend about 15 minutes coaching Jules doing soft toss pitch with him and then I'll come back to the office to continue to work for another hour or two to close up the office. He said yeah, okay, whatever you need to do. I really was disciplined with that. It didn't take long, I would drive home, the whole time I'm talking to myself and then I would say "Hey

Jules, come on. Let's go outside. Let's hit balls." And that's all we did, if you don't know what soft toss is, I would sit on a bucket and I would just throw balls up like about waist high from right next to him. And by the way, I'm terrible. I should probably never be the one pitching or throwing soft pitches.

As we began, some days he would be a typical little boy and say, "But Dad it's hot out, can I just play?" That was normal. I started softly tossing up balls and he's just swinging away. He missed some, but he hit some. When he connected I would say, that's awesome! Because it was cool to see him connect with a ball, even though it's soft toss. We just kept on doing that. And we would do it for about 15 minutes and what do you think happened some days? By the way, we never talked about keeping your eye on the ball, look at me, watch your toes, all those other coach's tips etc. I never gave him any pointers where to stand, how to hold the bat, choke up, put it by your ear, keep your bat right. None of that stuff. I would say "So hey, how was your day, what'd you guys learn? What'd you do in school? Who's bothering you bud?" We were just talking. Once I got him going he would just talk about his day and it was kind of cool just to hear about life from his perspective.

What do you think happened some days after about 15 minutes?

Yeah. Some days we would be there for like 30 minutes, we were just tossing the ball up, taking swings, hitting some and missing some. I had to do this timed with him because he grew up in this world, this generation. So usually after our 15 minutes, he would say, "Dad I really want to go inside and play video games!" Some days I would cave and say, oh all right, you can play video games. Just give me 15 minutes. Or he would say, Dad I need a drink of water. You get water in 15 minutes. We would sometimes go to 30. I think a couple of times we even went a full hour. We were just shooting the breeze, just the two of us.

The massive byproduct here is that it was an exceptional relationship building that I've never done before with my children. I just never did. Because I'm a driver! I'm always busy! I'm working! I'm trying to build!

I'm crushing things! Try not to lose sight of the reasons you started it all for in the beginning. By the way, a very special shout to my wife Angelique Brue, she was the one that always signed our children up for sports, she always made sure they everything they needed, and she would drive them to and from everything.

I didn't have to think about having those type of conversations. It happened naturally during this time we had together. After two weeks of doing this every day, game day comes along. It was my chance to once again put the 15 Minute Principle to the test let me see if this could work for something other than my CrossFit training. One night I arrive at the field and I'm late, of course. It's about 10 minutes into the game and I am on the phone, as usual, walking up to the field. I tell the person on the phone, listen, hang on one second. My son's up to bat. It's probably not going to be anything, but I should at least pay attention. I still remember who that agent was today because I screamed in her ear. That's why I know. She totally forgave me. Here I am giving her real estate advice and as I watch, he hits the ball.

He didn't just hit the ball a little bit, he crushed it. He hit the ball, I screamed it in this women's ear and I go running over. I'm shaking the field fence. I didn't even realize the chain link fence was shaking I was about ready to rip it right out. And here's my little boy rounding first, second, third wearing his cute little white baseball pants. He's rounding all the bases. I was having one of the greatest moments of my life.

It was like something you would've seen maybe in the World Series, well it was for me, it was massive. By the way, he didn't hit it over the fence, he actually hit the fence and he didn't get a home run. But he did get a triple, which was awesome. And of course, I was like, "Jules you could've made it home, you have just got to keep running." Totally me, right? But he listened to his coach because he is a great player and great players listen to their coaches.

But my point is this. He hit the ball, first ball, first pitch, no thinking. Hit it. At that moment I said to myself, you know what, this 15 minute thing is kind of working for me.

Then I had one other area in my life that it was kind of weak at that point in time. It was personal for me, so I won't get into all that with you because I don't want to take up your time for something personal like that. But it did help. I took 15 minutes every single day to actually invest in my personal relationships instead of just always focusing on myself and what I wanted. I just flipped it. The truth was I had to be purposeful and force myself to do it. Some days it's all I could do. 15 minutes and then I'm going to bounce. Tip never tell your family, spouse or significant other you are forcing yourself to do 15 minutes to work on the relationship.

At home with the family I would give 15 minutes of really good focus time. Asking questions and trying to really be present. I would ask how are you? What was on thing good that happened to each kid. Try to make it about the kids. So once again, my 15 Minute Principle is valid and worked.

But here's where I'm going to bring it back to you guys and I'm going to bring it back to business. I don't believe that your minds can handle lead generation time of three hours a day or even two hours a day. I am actually and totally convinced that for most of you, you can't sit still for one hour anymore. And I don't think it's anything wrong with you, it's not your fault. It's Apple's fault and Android platforms, these technologies changed the way we process info. It's truly not our fault, your brain processes like a computer with muscle memory. You swipe, you pinch, or you scroll. Our brains just are not programmed to have the ability to sit and focus for long periods of time for an hour or two hours or three hours. But try to start whatever it is you want to improve with just 15 minutes of initial focus time. You can do anything for 15 minutes and time and focus can regrow from there. Anytime my numbers got off track, I would simply go back to 15 minutes a day!

My Challenge To You

What I've decided to do is give you my biggest gift, which is my 15 Minute Principle and save you the heartache and pain from failing at whatever it is you want. So why don't you just try this thing of focus on the things you want most for 15 minutes every single day. If you can do 15 minutes every single day then I believe that you can probably live the kind of life you want. You can make the kind of money you want. I promise you, it will be a chore at first, but do it anyway, never miss a day when you are in the build. Do it for at least 90 days. Some of you are already challenging this, I call you, The Challengers. And you know what? I challenge you to challenge me and do the 15 minutes every single day. For 90 days, on purpose no distractions. The total focus should be on making contacts and appointments, to prove me wrong. Go ahead, try it! I challenge you! I know I can change your life with 15 minutes as a Principle!

I have had my best successes in life trying to prove my boss and now partner Charles Posess wrong. He's my boss so I have to do it, right? It's important sometimes to prove him wrong. I've gone way out of my way to prove him wrong and it backfires in a really good way. Because most of the times I end up growing our organization because I was so ultra-focused on growth to prove him wrong. A great byproduct that happens, you see, I wasn't often right, but my life got bigger and better. I was laser focused and fueled by trying to prove him wrong. So, if you do this, if you're just going to do it to challenge me and say I don't think it's going to work, I want you to, I accept your challenge. I want you to do the 15 minutes every single day, four days a week minimum, just like you would any good workout routine for your business. Do it for three months. At the end of three months if you're legitimate and you go 15 minutes every single day at the onset of the day, four days a week minimum, at the end of three months, then I will give you the ability to circle back to me and say that didn't work. Is that cool? Is that fair? Yep, because I know it will change your life!

I've been doing this now for 18 years. I have been on the leadership and management side of this business now for the past 15 years. We have built the absolute biggest enterprise in a single group of real estate franchises that anyone has built in Florida's history to date. And all that stuff is super cool. But what I've always done when we were not where we need to be, is, I would always come back to this very principle and start with making the commitment to put the first 15 minutes

I'm on in business all about growth, lead generation and creation!

I always review my big why goals, my big things I want to achieve, acquire or desire. Matter of fact, as I got older my toys got bigger, my appetite for success got larger and my need for more got deeper. I don't need more toys. What I found as you grow and metamorphose is your big why goals change and morph as you do. What I found was I would take my 15 Minute Principle and I would parlay it into every other aspect of my life.

As you implement the 15 Minute Principle into your life, other aspects where you're weak become identifiable, because let's face it, there are some places that you're weak and there are some places that you're strong. And if you really want to grow in those weak areas you might try putting that 15 Minute Principle towards it, before accepting defeat. Find out if it's something that you really care about, and you really want because if it's not, it's won't work anyway. Take that 15 minutes of your beautiful time and place it over there on something that you actually do want and desire and will matter, it will actually pay you dividends beyond what you first could conceive.

In my 18 years in this business with 15 of them on the leadership management side at Keller Williams. I've seen more agents graduate from new agent to mega agent than probably most brokers in Florida. Some agents make it, some don't, here's what I'm going to tell you. There is nothing that the agents who succeed at the level you want to succeed at have over anybody reading this book. They're not any better. They're not any taller. They're not any shorter, they're not any better looking. They're not better educated. They're not better dressed. They don't have better verbiage. They don't present better. They don't have better habits. They're just people like you and me.

> ## "You have to take action!"
>
> BRUE

And what they did was, they found fundamental principles like this that they were able to put in play for them and then they actually took action. You have to take the action. You can't just say you want it. You've got to actually go out and do it.

Conclusion

My close to you is this. Anything that you want to do in this life and business is totally available. You have the capabilities and the strengths inside you if you really want it. Find out what you really want and then come up with a business plan of what it looks like, be specific about what it is that you want to go after. Take a time block, cut the time, put it into some type of calendar. By the way, when I switched over to digital, those of you that are digital, it takes me about 20 minutes to do my whole calendar for the year and its color coordinated.

But if you're not, it takes a couple hours when you're doing it the old school way like I used to do in a planner.

I had a student ask me about lead generation specifically and they said, "Do you dedicate so much time to certain areas. As in, do you break it down so that you dedicate so much time to cold calls, so much time to expireds, so much time to marketing in the area? Or do you just take that 15 minutes and lump it all together for that that day?"

That's a beautiful question. What I would do is find out what your strengths are and what you're good at and then do more of those. I find that if you're deathly afraid of something, like cold calling, you will get really nervous about it. You won't want to do it and you'll actually hide from it and run from it. If I were to make that mandatory or I try to push you to do it, there's always going to be that resistance. So, I would rather focus on what you will do rather than what we both know you won't.

I believe they all work, everything works. I think you can actually build a whole real estate practice around social media if you're good enough and you're smart about building the right audience and learn to connect with them while you're building the right relationships through social media.

You can call for sale by owners. You can call expireds. There are people who still call for sale by owners. People that are in your sphere of influence. I happen to think the sphere of influence is probably the one that will take you the farthest and the deepest as quick as possible. You just have to understand that your sphere of influence is not one level deep. It's actually multiple levels deep.

Let's look at an example of how your sphere of influence is actually multiple levels deep. Let's take my friend Nadia. She's in my first level friend circle. But she knows this guy Steve and I don't really know that guy. I've been eyeing him and stuff and I know he looks cool but I'm not sure about him. But she knows him. What I'm going to do is be able to leverage the relationship I have with Nadia to develop a better relationship with Steve. She'll probably bridge the gap at least once. We'll be at a party or some gathering, and the opportunity will present itself.

Now let's take it a step further, Steve has a friend Francine and she does not know me from Adam. I'm the third party removed but somehow you get invited into this networking thing. We're all there at a party together and now all of a sudden because of my first friend, I've got two and three levels deep. You see how that works.

The sphere of influence is something that I would probably focus on or at least be at the forefront of everything that we do because it will pay the most dividends the longest.

I think they all work. I am of the belief that no matter what it is, it works. If you want to farm a neighborhood and you send enough postcards and enough marketing and you have the cash to do that, you're going to be successful. You just have to do it long enough for your return and investment to come back.

A couple key points on that. If you're going to farm an area, make sure that you are sending as frequent as the other people, your competitors are sending. If they're sending once a month, you've got to send once a month. If they send once a month and you send once a year, you're going to just waste the money. That's not farming, that's fishing. If they go 12 a year, you go 12 a year. If they have jumbo postcards with beautiful pictures on them and there are just incredible skylines and everything else, well then, your postcards better look just as good. You can't send black and white little tiny ones just to say you're in the game. You have got to mirror them. At least go to the level that the competition is doing or more.

I think everything works if you apply yourself and make it work.

Now I want you, yes you, reading this book right now, I want you to take it and actually do this. I want your feedback. I want you to send me a message in three months from now and share with me results only if you actually did this on purpose. I want to hear from you, the new next level you, I'm making six million a year and it's just a crazy new big life and I'm driving this fancy car or that badass truck, I smashed my goals by more than double, I'm taking my dream vacation this year to some exotic place. I want to hear about it. What or who do you become?

To your success. I believe in you and my greatest hope is that one day you see your beautiful self through my eyes.

Michael

About *"The General"* Michael Brue

Michael Brue specializes in helping professional's break down the walls of mediocrity and get on a proven path to growth and success. His life work is helping people meet their maximum future self!

He has been a top Real Estate Broker and General Manager for close to 15 years using his expertise to help build and expand his five Keller Williams Realty Market Centers in South Florida. Michael leads a team of 1,100 plus Realtors© spread across five market centers and two supporting business centers that have generated several billion dollars in volume. He is passionate about building others up and allowing them to shine with the success he knows is inside of them.

Using his proven system, he is able to draw out an agent's maximum potential.

KW Palm Beaches, KW Jupiter, KW Treasure Coast, KW Palm City, KW Port St Lucie, KW Vero Beach and the Island of Vero Beach.

Made in the USA
Columbia, SC
03 July 2018